THE SCIENCE OF PEOPLE PERFORMANCE

Tool Kit for XO Performers

Nishant Kumar Gautam & Prim Farim

INDIA · SINGAPORE · MALAYSIA

ISBN 979-8-88641-575-9

NISHANT KUMAR GAUTAM

Mr. Nishant is the Chairman of All India Corporate Council for Skill Development. An educator, business management consultant and a life-skills coach, he is a much sought-after speaker. His 20+ years of learning and experience have helped organizations navigate their journey through work and workforce transformation.

He has helped thousands of people across the globe transform their lives and their businesses through his programs, workshops, seminars and personal coaching. As an advisor for several leading technical and management institutions and corporates, he has helped them in maximizing growth and improving business performance. He has donned multiple hats and played diverse roles in his professional career of over two decades.

PRIM FARIM

Mr. Prim is the founder/CEO of Dibta Group and Lead Coach at Dibta Indonesia. Prim started his career at Motorola and spent 25 years across diverse platforms, ranging from technical to management roles. In 2002, he joined Maybank Corporation as their Chief Learning Officer, to lead and transform their corporate university. In 2004, he started Dibta Group globally, with offices across Asia and has pioneered several corporate learning and leadership innovations. He is currently working on developing the next-generation organization learning technology for the establishment of Corporate University 4.0.

Prim has conducted workshops, coached, facilitated learning and developed learning systems across Asia, the USA and Europe. His models are utilized by many learning technologists globally. Prim has also chaired, mediated and presented at many conferences globally, including IFTDO and CIPD.

Preface

"Knowing yourself is the beginning of all wisdom."

– Aristotle

My role as a consultant over the past two decades has offered me great exposure to work with diverse professionals. In this journey, I have come across many case studies of individuals and enterprises. Each one of them had their own share of success and failure. What I observed as a common trait in the success stories was how these professionals learnt from their mistakes and did not let their failures overwhelm them when they needed their inner strength. While many people and systems played important roles in their successes and failures, it was purely their individual strength and mastery of self that determined their path to success or failure.

During this time, I met Mr. Prim at a conference in Indonesia. My presentation on People's Performance impressed him. His vast experience in learning organization gave me insights into large-scale transformations. We struck a chord instantly and recognized our complementary strengths. Ever since, we have been working together on taking our experiences and learnings to large audiences through seminars, workshops and conferences.

But we knew deep in our hearts that it was not enough. This learning must be reinforced at one's own convenience, providing the reader the time to learn, apply and learn again.

It requires acceptance and commitment from individuals to make that change. That is when the idea of writing this book was conceptualized. This book is purely organized and written based on our series of lectures and facilitation sessions. If someone is willing to spend a few hours for the sake of self-development — on reading, immersing and absorbing information by perusing this book — then we have hit the bull's eye.

This book is an attempt to navigate the reader through the core concepts of personal transformation and support them in the implementation of these concepts with the help of simple tools and techniques. The concepts help to understand the reasoning, the value, the importance, the relevance and the outcome of every suggested action. The tools are self-help manuals that provide a simple way of applying these in every action. These tools, when implemented daily in various facets of life and course corrections duly made, will undoubtedly make the individual mightier.

In this sincere work derived from our vast experience, Prim and I provide individuals, students, entrepreneurs, teams and everyone else with the tools they can use to maximize potential in themselves and others. Whether you are starting up a new boutique firm, pursuing career growth, coaching football or teaching your child to play guitar, this book will provide guidance on enhancing your performance by tapping into scientific models through deep learning.

Before you start reading this book, note down WHAT is the ultimate thing you want to achieve. Belief is the essence of self-transformation. Now, take the first BIG and important step of BELIEVING IN YOURSELF. So why wait? Complete this book and discover yourself. We really hope that you will enjoy reading this book as much as we enjoyed putting it together. We hope it helps you realize a meaningful outcome.

"Faith is taking the first step, even when you don't see the whole staircase."

– Martin Luther

Acknowledgments

Having an idea and turning it into a book is more challenging than I thought and more rewarding than I could have ever imagined. The book would not be a reality without my mentor, Mr. Prim. He is the inspiration and foundation behind the journey of penning down my experiences in the form of this book. Prim, thank you for being my Guru, whom I trust, honor and respect. Any accomplishment is the outcome of the sacrifices and effort of many people, and this work is no different.

Firstly, I would like to thank my father Sri Shailendra Kumar Singh and mother Smt. Asha Singh, whose upbringing gave me the core values and principles of my life. Without their blessings, I would not have achieved anything.

I would like to thank my wife Anitha, my son Aman and my daughter Nidhi, whose patience and support were instrumental in accomplishing this task.

My heartfelt thanks to my siblings, relatives, teachers and my dearest friends for their constant support and encouragement.

My sincere gratitude to the thousands of people who attended my workshops and seminars, without whom there would be no 'The Science of People of Performance.'

I would also like to thank the valuable contributions of all the reviewers, whose diligent efforts made this publication possible.

A few examples, stories and anecdotes are the result of collection from various sources, such as newspapers, magazines, other speakers and seminar participants over the past twenty years. Unfortunately, sources were not always noted or available. Regardless of the source, I wish to acknowledge those who have contributed to this work, even though anonymously.

And above all, I would like to thank the ALMIGHTY for guiding me in the right direction and empowering me with the belief that I CAN.

— **Nishant Kumar Gautam**

Dedicated to

Samuel Navamani Nadar

(My late father who taught me how to LOVE,
LEARN and LEAD despite all conditions)

Prim Farim

Through this book, I would like to thank all the teachers in my life who directly or indirectly have helped me shape my life and learn that "LIFE is about living, and LOVE is about giving." I would like to acknowledge,

- Madam Leela, my mother who taught me about hard work and perseverance

- Mr. Philip, who rewarded me with my first fountain pen at a time when I could not even afford to buy pencils

- Miss Tang, my secondary school teacher who trusted me and let me lead my first project

- Pastor Allan, who gave me the first opportunity to teach at the church fellowship group

- Mr. Lee, who offered me part-time employment to supplement my family income

- Uncle Maniam, who paid my Cambridge secondary examination fee

- Mr. Kana and Mr. Queck for hiring me into Motorola

- Mr. Cheah, for mentoring me to be a trainer at Motorola

- Uztaz Ibrahim, for his wisdom that inspired me to make a difference in my life

- Miss Mary Kennedy, for providing opportunity to lead the Training Department at Motorola Malaysia

- Mr. Stephen Kremple, for teaching the basics of organization learning technology

- Mr. Bill Wiggenhorn, for providing regional opportunity at Motorola University

- Miss Jennifer, for helping me expand into China's corporate learning business

- Mr. Honglei and Mr. Jincheng, for assisting me through my corporate teacher life

- Mr. Zuber, for helping me sustain when my business went through turmoil

- Mr. Liew, for providing opportunity to teach at the CCP Leadership School

- Mr. Steven Yudiyanto, for helping me build my first corporate university in Indonesia

- Ibu Anna Maria and Sinta Maharani, for introducing and institutionalizing corporate universities in Indonesia

- Mr. Nishant, for helping me with Dibta's corporate university initiatives as Principal Consultant

- Julia Ahmad, my loving wife who inspired and supported me throughout my life, to seek and find the "pot of gold" at the end of my rainbow

Once a fisherman at sea, refused to accept money when I requested some small fishes as baits and taught me a rule that fishermen follow — "while at the sea, the more you give out, the more the sea will give back you."

My life has been so — the more I have taught, the more I have learnt from those whom I have taught, and I hope to continue this till the end of my life.

I sincerely pray and wish that this book would make a difference in your life's journey.

– Prim Farim

Contents

Part 1

Understanding Personal Transformation

Chapter 1

Personal Mastery Model and Deep Learning

"If we don't change, we don't grow.
If we don't grow, we aren't really living."

– Gail Sheehy

If you look around yourself, you will notice that in nature everything is either growing or dying. The leaves on the plants grow, perform photosynthesis, change their color and look beautiful, even when they are not synthesizing any food; then, they dry and fall off. The cycle of change and growth repeats. When there is no change happening, the leaves die.

Even our relationships, businesses and health start receding and dying if they are not replenished, maintained and grown. What this means is it is constant progress and growth that keep all of these alive.

Humans are not meant to stop growing either. Progress in life is all about transformation, which provides us opportunities to explore ourselves and change. Here, change is not outward facing but inward. We can't always control external people and events, but we can change ourselves. And the best thing is that everything changes when you change yourself.

There cannot be a better example than the story of the Father of the Nation, Gandhiji, who attained personal transformation. Gandhiji was thrown out of a first-class train compartment in Pietermaritzburg, South Africa, because he was colored. That moment brought out the inner desire and drive within Gandhiji that defined the rest of his life and that of an entire nation. Gandhiji went through self-transformation and changed from within, without any external agent or support.

Personal transformation is all about becoming aware and knowledgeable about your actions and the drive behind them and, then, accepting the truth about your actions, making the required changes and, finally, reinforcing the shift in your actions by recognizing and rewarding yourself.

Transformation is a deep process and not a quick-fix solution. It is a deliberate and constant practice with a purpose that involves a cycle of distinct actions.

What drives personal transformation?

In the case of Gandhiji or any other extraordinary achievers, it was always their powerful goals that drove their transformation. If you reflect on your life as well, you will realize that your moments of success and achievements were determined by your ultimate goals or desires that you held.

"Every success story is a tale of constant adaption, revision and change."

– Richard Branson

For more than 70 years, runners had been chasing the elusive goal of running one mile under four minutes. In

1954, Sir Roger Bannister achieved this goal and became the first athlete to finish one mile under four minutes — at 3 minutes 59.4 seconds. He held this record for a mere 46 days, when John Landy became the second athlete to finish at a record time of 3 minutes 58 seconds. A feat that took years to achieve for Roger Bannister was broken in just 46 days by Landy. It did not remain a remarkable record for very long. Over the next few years, more runners broke the four-minute mark.

How did Roger Bannister do it? And how did many others achieve the same result subsequently?

Roger Bannister did not follow conventional models of training and coaching. Instead, he formulated his own methods to prepare for the race. When no one believed his goals were possible, he did. When he failed publicly, he picked himself up and moved on. He took things into his own hands and decided to tell the world a better story. And in doing so, he did the impossible.

Prior to the 1968 Olympics, the Olympic record for men's high jump was less than 2.18 meters. In the 1968 event in Mexico City, America's Dick Fosbury won the gold medal by achieving a height of 2.24 meters. Fosbury created history in this event by using an unprecedented style of jumping (a backward flip), which later came to be called the Fosbury Flop. In the following years, Fosbury Flop became the standard style used in high jump.

When Bannister broke the running record, other runners received a clear signal that they could do it too, and suddenly, everyone was able to do it. When Fosbury used a new jumping style, he set the precedent and his style became the standard. These stories provide an important lesson — "Once you stop believing something is impossible, it becomes possible."

These stories can inspire us all — career aspirants, students, leaders in organizations, entrepreneurs, researchers, everyone. One innovator changes the game, and that which was thought unreachable becomes a benchmark for the rest. That is Roger Bannister's and Dick Fosbury's true legacy and lesson for all of us. We need to see success as believing in oneself and doing things that haven't been done before.

From the above stories, we see that everything Bannister and Fosbury thought and did, culminated into their record-breaking performances.

We can therefore conclude that:

PERFORMANCE = ACTION + THINKING

To achieve the right performance, right thinking and right action are always required. To understand and master this, we need to look deeper within ourselves, and we need to look at it from the core of our beings.

DEEP PERFORMANCE is a combination of five stages within us. It starts with our DRIVE, INTENTION and BELIEF, which play a big role in our THINKING and ACTION.

Our thinking and action will affect what we SAY and DO, resulting in our performance.

The source of our actions is our thinking. Be it home or workplace, our thoughts drive our actions. Then, what exactly drives our thoughts? What makes us think the way we think? Is there something beyond thinking?

In our day-to-day lives, we come across several experiences, references, as well as examples. We interpret these and form our opinions and convictions accordingly. This is what BELIEF is. Beliefs are chosen based on our experiences. Thinking is manifested by our beliefs. At the surface level, actions are driven by thinking and thinking is driven by beliefs, which are ingrained deep within us.

If we thrust the beliefs of others upon us, then naturally our thinking and action change accordingly. So, if others don't believe we can achieve our goals, then we also begin to believe it.

But aren't beliefs that are at the core of our thinking and action supposed to be our own? Yes! Hence, it is very important to choose the right beliefs for ourselves. To do that, we need to know what influences the way we choose our beliefs.

Let us examine this with an example. When we struggle to work with our manager, we tend to believe that he is not a good manager. This belief is driven by a selective memory of negative experiences with our manager. It ignores all the positive experiences we shared. Why is it so? Why do we tend to choose only certain beliefs and reject others?

This is where the concept of INTENTION comes in. We choose our beliefs to support our intentions. In the above example, the intention is to prove that our struggle at work is the manager's fault. Hence, all our beliefs stem out of negative experiences that reinforce that intention.

Now, the question is why we intend that way. There must be something beyond intention that controls and influences one's intention. When explored further, desire was found to be the controlling factor. What lies beyond intention is DESIRE.

Desire is a strong feeling of wanting to have something or wishing for something to happen. But many times, desire is instinctive. Desire needs to be mastered, managed and directed, and then, it becomes DRIVE.

"DESIRE MASTERED IS DRIVE"

In the example discussed, our drive is the fear of losing our job. This fear drives our intention negatively to prove ourselves right and our manager wrong. Hence, our belief system selectively chooses only the negative experiences with the manager and, eventually, these thoughts drive our actions towards reacting negatively with our manager. The connection between these concepts is the foundation of the Personal Mastery Model.

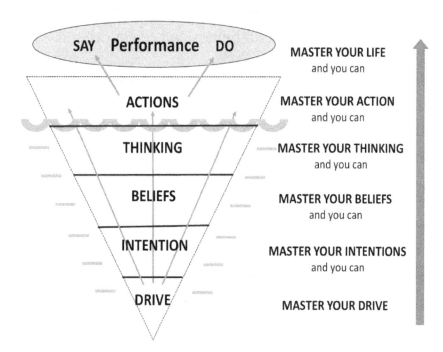

If we master our drive, we will be able to master our intention, beliefs, thinking and actions. So, in a way, if we master our drive, we can triumphantly master everything in our life. Giving direction to one's drive is the essence of this book.

"What lies behind us and what lies before us are tiny matters compared to what lies within us."

– Ralph Waldo Emerson

DRIVE

"If you limit your choices only to what seems possible or reasonable, you disconnect yourself from what you truly want, and all that is left is a compromise."

– Robert Fritz

Every activity of an individual must begin with the inner DRIVE, which will end up influencing the INTENTION. What we intend will control the selection of our BELIEFS, and these beliefs will help shape our THINKING. Thinking will ultimately manifest as our ACTIONS, which then will determine our performance (the results, the output, the outcome, etc.). This is the foundation that transforms individuals, teams and organizations through the concept of deep learning.

Drive can be defined as a desire to achieve and a passion to strive for the best. Drive is the basic spiritual purpose of an individual that is beyond one's physical, emotional and social needs. This "spiritual need" differentiates humans from the rest of the living beings. Drive can be influenced by various factors — love, expectation of respect, fear of loss, anger, hope, aspiration to power, revenge, grief, sense of urgency and passion to excel. It holds the key to our performance. Drive provides us the required energy and motivation — "YES, I CAN DO IT!" With proper drive, individuals will be able to shape their intention. Let us understand this in detail. How do we give direction to our vision and desire?

Subconscious: Discover the garden of your life

Often people tend to think that one's vision is one's blueprint for the future. This is what our subconscious mind thinks we want and uses it to shape our life. But have you ever wondered whether the vision that popped up in your mind is really what you want? Our subconscious mind is like an unkempt garden, and we are the gardeners responsible for beautifying it. Our subconscious mind grows either flowers or weeds in the garden, whichever we plant. Hence, we must plant what we want in terms of our goals and desires.

We will need a crystal-clear idea of what is important to us and what we want. This is a crucial point because our subconscious mind is responsible for manifesting our vision and directing our focus. The more we fix our minds on what we want, the faster it happens. This process keeps our mind away from what we don't want. The greater the rapport between our normal awareness and our subconscious mind, the higher the ability to master our drive.

If your life is lacking in some areas, it is likely that you have conflicting desires (e.g., "I want to lose weight, but I don't want to change my diet"), or maybe because you don't believe it is possible.

To get a clear understanding of what you want in your life, begin by writing down the vision for your life. Go with the flow and let your subconscious unveil point wise what you want your life to be like. Don't edit anything. Don't worry about what is possible, realistic or right. Your priority is to gain clarity on the 'what' first, not the 'how'. The how will follow along the way when you start taking actions. For now, focus on the WHAT, and the direction to your vision and desire.

INTENTION

"Have the courage to follow your heart and intuition. They somehow already know what you truly want to become. Everything else is secondary."

– Steve Jobs

Intention is the 'purpose' that you plan and intend to carry out. It's important to know 'where' you want to go and 'why' you desire it. When you decide to do something, it starts with an intention. Intention is the primary instinctive purpose for one to choose and live upon a particular belief. When you set the right intention, it manifests your beliefs and fuels your passion towards performance.

Start questioning your intent repeatedly so that you get to know the real intent for your desire/drive. This can be done using the 5 Whys approach.

5 Whys

The basic definition of intention itself is the 'why' question — Why does someone go to office every day, even when they do not like the job? Why does the job matter to an individual? To know your intention behind anything, capture why you are doing it. For example, let us think about a scenario of you wanting to start a business.

Rewrite the questions and answers as shown in the figure below:

Hence, offering SERVICE to the needy in society is your DRIVE to start a new business. This requires you to look inside and be committed to the truth. You must clearly know the reason behind your intent or purpose; only then you will be able to know your DRIVE.

BELIEF

"All things splendid have been achieved by those who dared believe that something inside them was superior to circumstance."

– Bruce Barton

Belief is an idea or thought that we accept as true or real. Once we form an opinion that our beliefs are true, we will persistently hold onto them, regardless of the impact these may have on us or those around us. This is because a belief is the ultimate strength of our intentions. They are the Programs and Scripts that one has either consciously or unconsciously selected, accepted and coded into one's mind, which conditions and structures one's thinking. It is a feeling of rigidity, permanence, certainty, confidence and assurance. An individual's being is incomplete without a belief.

Beliefs originate and ripen gradually with passing time. Over the years, we acquire a set of beliefs through the way we live our lives and the interpretations we make of our past experiences. Why do we think the way we think? It is because of past experiences. We need to start believing in ourselves by disproving negative thoughts that originated from our past experiences, opinions and convictions. We need to develop a fresh outlook by cleansing our minds of the negative thoughts that cloud it.

Let us think about a scenario. If you believe you are not good at sports, ask yourself, "Am I really not good at any sports?" The answer will reveal itself to you. It might be that you are better in some sports than others, or it might also be that you haven't played many of them. Then, why do you make it a permanent belief that you are not good at any sports at all?

In this scenario, your real intention is to not play any sports; hence, you tend to choose only those negative beliefs and experiences that support your intention of not playing any sports. It ignores all the positive beliefs such as 'you have chosen not to play many sports; hence, you are not good at them either.'

Always question the intention to disprove your negative belief system that is socially conditioned by negative experiences and negative interpretations. This will give you the ability to work towards your new positive belief system.

Self-confidence

Belief system has a major impact on one's self-confidence. Many of us do not even believe that we are worthy of possessing what we truly desire. This is because our self-confidence becomes rusted by our doubts, fears and self-criticism. Another reason for lack of confidence in ourselves is that we get negatively influenced by our circumstances, and we consider them unchangeable and rigid.

For instance, you feel painfully stuck and suffocated in a job you don't love. You develop a lot of reasons and excuses for not finding a better opportunity. But what you don't have is just the confidence to solve the problem. Your feelings and reactions to situations emerge from your thoughts and beliefs about your circumstances, not directly from the circumstances themselves. Refuse to believe that things will never change. Instead, believe in your ability to change yourself and your circumstances.

Your level of self-confidence drives your choices and behaviors, which explains why sometimes you move ahead, sometimes you are stagnant in a place and sometimes you even fall behind.

Think about what changes you would like to make in your life, and then, think about whether you have the confidence to make those changes. It is rigid beliefs that lay the foundation of self-confidence. A self-confident person can achieve harder things than a talented person who lacks self-confidence. Believing in yourself is crucial to move to higher levels in life and achieve ultimate success.

THINKING

"Thinking is progress. Non-thinking is stagnation of the individual, organization and the country. Thinking leads to action. Knowledge without action is useless and irrelevant. Knowledge with action converts adversity into prosperity."

– Dr. A. P. J. Abdul Kalam

The mindset or the ability to think big plays a key role in one's journey towards success. If a company called Apple could bloom from a tiny garage into a multi-billion-dollar technology company, why not think that all dreams can come true? For the sake of argument, if we assume that dreams are at times like mirages and impossible to get hold of, the least we can do is chase them with grit and determination. A positive mindset allows us to overcome hardships to chase our dreams. A negative mindset throws various barriers, making us believe that our dreams are impossible.

Thinking is the process of using our minds to produce ideas. It is the first order of occurrence that motivates our action. It is the mind maps and flow of thoughts that trigger, influence and manifest as the identified actions. One needs to confront and question themselves on their views, opinions, perspectives and approach to problem solving. Only when we do this, we start thinking about moving away from our past negative beliefs, ideas and behaviors, and towards our future goals, dreams and desires.

Our thinking makes up who we are and what we set out to do. When we think we can, we will see it in our actions. We master our lives by mastering how we think because ultimately our thoughts create the outcomes in our lives. Thinking will manifest the actions.

Indulging in positive self-talk can help us clarify our thought processes.

Self-talk

Self-talk is a combination of our ongoing thoughts and inner communication. We know that how we communicate with others is critical, but what about how we communicate with ourselves? Self-talk is the foundation upon which we build everything else. This is about scripting our thoughts to formulate our beliefs. Our self-talk explains why we take actions on some things and procrastinate acting on others. "You literally talk yourself into something, or you talk yourself out of it."

Let us take an example. If you think about what you really want in life and tell yourself that you know how to achieve it, then you are talking yourself into something you want. But if you tell yourself that what you want is not realistic, you will talk yourself out of what you want.

If you compliment yourself, you will feel good; if you criticize yourself, you will feel bad. Tell yourself you can do something, and you are more likely to succeed; tell yourself you can't, and you are more likely to fail.

Self-talk affects everything from how you feel to what you do or don't do. Developing the ability of proper self-talk will remove the thick clouds of doubt completely from your mind. By mastering your self-talk, you will be able to act much quicker and be more resilient.

"We are sum total of our own thoughts."

– Earl Nightingale

ACTION

"Courage is not the absence of fear; it is the decision that something else is far more important than the fear itself!"

– Ambrose Redmoon

When we were young, we sought validation for our actions from parents and family; later, from our teachers and friends, and eventually, our peers and managers. We always depend on external validation for our actions. Personal Mastery involves a shift from external validation to internal validation. This doesn't mean that we don't care about what others think. It only means that we give more importance to our thoughts and beliefs. This liberates us to do what is truly important to us and to live our dreams and desires, which originate from our inner drive. When we change the way we think, we will be able to change the way we act. Action is nothing but what one says or does, including verbal outputs, facial gestures and physical movements. Action will affect what we SAY and DO, determining our performance.

However, we know that making the change (action) takes a long time. What we don't realize is that:

"If you keep doing what you have always done, you keep getting what you have always got."

– Tony Robbins

Hence, massive actions play an important role in change. For example, if you want to be healthy, then you have to take massive action to make that change. Remove everything that is unhealthy from your refrigerator, strap on your running shoes and start off with your healthy routine. You cannot procrastinate things and still expect results. Every time you set a goal, take at least one immediate action towards its attainment.

Eisenhower prioritization/decision matrix

Now that you know how actions are manifested from your thinking, start introspecting into your actions, to decide on focus areas to improve the quality of your performance. Prepare your to-do list — big or small — that will move you closer to what you want. Next, prioritize your list. The prioritization/decision matrix, shown in the figure, is a tool that will help you categorize your actions by order of priority as Important, Not Important, Urgent and Not Urgent.

- Category I — Urgent and Important

- Category II — Not Urgent but Important

- Category III — Not Important but Urgent

- Category IV — Not Important and Not Urgent

	Urgent	Not Urgent
Important	I DO	II PLAN
Not Important	III DELEGATE	IV ELIMINATE

CONSUMING

EFFECTIVE

INEFFECTIVE

Category II items are the most important ones for your life. This is where you should spend maximum time. This category has all the actions that require planning — long term, short term and everything in between. Health, family, work, study — everything needs adequate planning. Spend maximum time here to plan your actions, looking forward. This will eliminate crisis mode as much as possible and keep you focused on what you should be doing at a given time.

Category I items are those that need immediate action. The actions here should follow from your plan from Category II items. These must be done by you at that time. They consume the highest energy. They can also be crisis actions. These cannot be eliminated completely but can be kept under control by proper planning. Avoid adding items to this list that haven't followed from Category II.

Category III items are those that come up suddenly but can be delegated or postponed. Some people spend time in

Category III thinking they are in Category I. The items in this category are likely to be important to someone else but not to you.

Category IV items are those that should be eliminated completely from your life. Nothing constructive happens here.

Effective people stay out of Category III and IV and focus on increasing Category II while shrinking Category I. You can increase the Category II items and decrease Category I by managing your time and energy.

But TIME is a finite resource and available in equal quantity for all. What is not finite is the ENERGY within you. Energy is the capacity to do work and is derived from your body, emotions, mind and spirit. The state of each of these four variables defines the energy you carry within; energy can be renewed to the fullest by properly managing it. The greater the positivity in these four entities, the greater is the positive energy. You must always try to maintain a healthy body and a healthy mind by performing yoga, exercising and practicing meditation.

Identify the energy suckers in your routine — behaviors, activities — and get rid of them as soon as you can. Start your day keeping track of the end in your mind. List your daily activities/tasks and categorize them as Category I, II, III and IV, according to the matrix. Review your priority list and energy sucker list every day, take action and monitor your progress for improved performance.

"Growth is painful. Change is painful. But nothing is as painful as staying stuck where you do not belong."

– N. R. Narayana Murthy

ACTION TO DRIVE — DEEP LEARNING ANALYSIS

"He who controls others may be powerful, but he who has mastered himself is mightier still."

– Lao Tzu

You have now learnt what is the ultimate desire/drive that manifests as your actions, and you have also learnt how to give directions to your actions to achieve meaningful outcomes. It is now time to introspect and make course corrections through deep learning. Discovering the self is not good enough, you need to realize and transform.

Deep learning analysis helps you uncover and identify the invisible force that conducts and controls your personal behavior. It will venture deep into your soul to explore and embrace the "truth" behind your every action and reaction, so that you master and manage them.

For every action, list down the thinking, beliefs and intention behind it in the sequence of 1-2-3-4. This will help you unveil your desire and drive.

1. What was exactly "said and done" by me?

2. What was my "real" thinking when I said or performed those actions?

3. What was my "actual" belief that caused me to think that way?

4. What was my "personal" intention that prompted me to select and accept that belief?

5. What was the "Instinctive Drive" that justified the intention?

Then, start questioning: "What is your action for?" Is it because of love or respect or fear for the person? If it was because of fear and now you want to transform it to love, then you must start the reverse process. Start questioning and listing down in sequence of 7-8-9-10 your intentions, thinking, beliefs and, finally, the expected action, which will be altered.

6. What should be the "Appropriate Drive" that can nurture the "Right Intention"?

7. What should be the "Right Intention" that allows me to select the "Positive Beliefs"?

8. What should be the "Positive Belief" that will govern the needed "Thinking"?

9. What should be the "Right Thinking" that can manifest as the "Appropriate Action"?

10. What should be the most "Appropriate Action" that can result in the "Desired Performance"?

Here, you have moved from actions due to fear for a person TO actions due to love for a person. This is the transformation through realization of your drive.

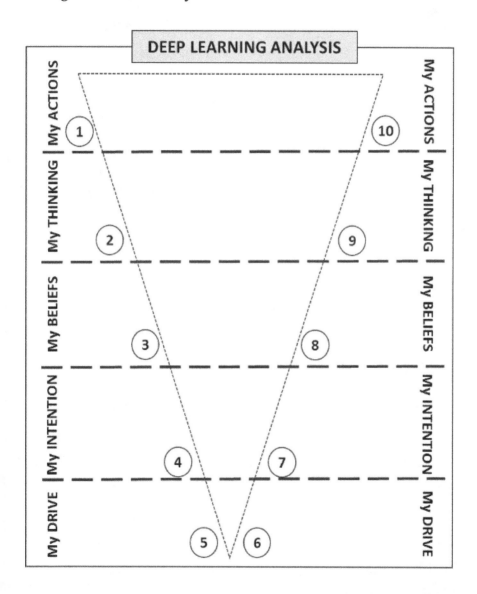

Let us understand this with a simple example of how to move from poor performance to extraordinary performance by realizing your DRIVE, while all other external factors remain the same.

Deep Learning Analysis (As Is)		Deep Learning Analysis (Should Be)	
My ACTION	Procrastinate & deliver Poor Results	Adhere to plan & deliver Excellent Results	My ACTION
My THINKING	There is no time to read and its not easy to score marks	Have to make time to get maximum reading hours, and for this one should plan the day, eliminate waste	My THINKING
My BELIEFS	Parents are bossy and try to enforce control	Appreciate the concerns and sacrifices of my Parents	My BELIEFS
My INTENTION	Pretend as reading just to make Parents feel better	To give ones best to keep Parents Happy	My INTENTION
My DRIVE	Fear of Parents	Love and Respect for Parents	My DRIVE

Summary

Achieving personal mastery is all about how one can manage and direct the driving force of their life, thus taking care of all their intentions, beliefs, thinking and actions. Using the approach and tools listed in this chapter, you will be able to scientifically define WHAT you want, WHERE you want to go and HOW you want to achieve sustainable performance and, eventually, realize and transform yourself.

Part 2

Applying Personal Transformation Principles for Enhanced Performance

Chapter 2

Extra-Ordinary (XO) Performance

"Respect, recognition, and reward flow out of performance."

– N. R. Narayana Murthy

Most of my programs and workshops are activity oriented and the insights that I get each time I interact with different groups is always new and refreshing. Almost in every event or game that is conducted, I see mixed responses and engagement by participants. I observed that the participants have different dispositions and attitude towards the whole exercise. When categorized, they fell under four types with differing momentum and drive to complete the activity.

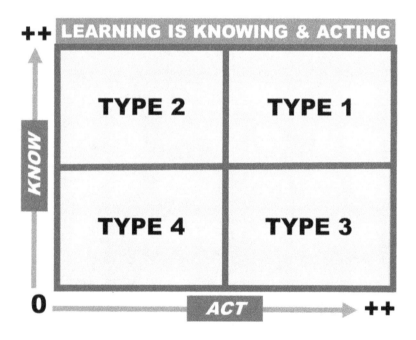

TYPE 1 group is not hesitant and is fully energized to go all out to enjoy. They understand all the key instructions and act immediately with prime focus on the task. They love to explore and adapt to the changing environment around them. They focus on maximizing the opportunity with the available resources and capabilities.

TYPE 2 group is hesitant and wait to be approached by others. They are so focused on understanding all instructions in detail and reconfirming on several questions that they will have limited time to act on the task. This group is not assertive but very responsive; in spite of having similar understanding of the task like TYPE 1, this group generally will fail to deliver what is expected out of them simply because they do not act fast. Unlike TYPE 1 people who are proactive, these are very reactive and like to remain in their comfort zone.

TYPE 3 group is proactive, involved and fully energized but lack complete understanding of what's happening around them. They participate just for the sake of it. They won't concentrate on the instructions given and they accept the changes readily without any questions.

TYPE 4 group is the most disengaged group and just stands wondering what is happening around them. They will be puzzled and won't even participate for the fear of NOT KNOWING what is transpiring. They probably misunderstand the instructions or do not pay attention when the instruction is given. Because of this they appear weak and dormant.

In retrospect, the groups can be compared to differing qualities of performance.

- TYPE 1 are the EXTRAORDINARY performers. They know what is required and are quick. They are committed to doing things, finding all reasons to achieve and innovating throughout.

- TYPE 2 are EXCELLENT performers who are innovators but lack focus and timely action and, eventually, end up not achieving their objectives.

- TYPE 3 are EXPECTED/ORDINARY performers who are proactive and do only as directed. They are not thought leaders and do not drive any innovations.

- TYPE 4 are POOR performers who lack both knowledge and action. They always find reasons for not performing.

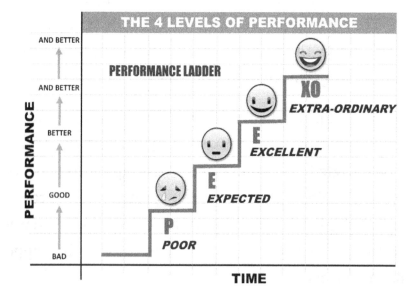

An EXCELLENT performer can achieve the best possible performance BECAUSE OF various favorable reasons, whereas an EXTRAORDINARY performer is able to achieve the best possible performance IN SPITE OF numerous constraints.

In the upcoming chapters you will learn how to apply the principles of Personal Mastery using various tools and master your performance TO BECOME EXTRAORDINARY, at least most of the time.

Chapter 3

5A's of Learning Cycle

"The best investment you can make is in yourself. The more you learn, the more you earn."

– Warren Buffett

LEARNING

Everyone probably remembers their first day at a new job, the first day of their first project. It is always an exciting journey in the first week. But after a few weeks if you continue to do the same things, you get bored and become stagnant. Initially, it is stimulating as you are learning new things and are progressing. The moment you stop learning or you get complacent, boredom sets in. If you see successful people like Steve Jobs, Bill Gates or anyone around you, you will notice that they are always curious, they never stop learning. It is the progress that they achieve from learning that keeps them happy and lively. This is also the driving force behind their mastery over self.

The first step towards personal mastery is LEARNING. But how does one understand and develop it? Can this be accomplished by mere reading of articles and books? Is it really that easy to attain? Or is there something beyond? If you opt to learn by buying a book or by attending a workshop, you have gained some knowledge. But you have not acquired any learning in the true sense. Knowledge by itself is empty, unless applied. For knowledge to become powerful, you must convert the knowledge into action at a very fast pace.

Learning is beyond reading, knowing and understanding. It is the ability to know, understand and address problems quickly.

READING ABILITY TO <u>KNOW</u> THERE IS A PROBLEM

KNOWING ABILITY TO <u>UNDERSTAND</u> THE PROBLEM

LEARNING ABILITY TO <u>ADDRESS</u> THE PROBLEM

UNLEARNING

You must have come across the buzz word 'continuous learning'. How will you learn continuously? If we look at traditional ways of learning, we will find that it was all about adding more information. While this might build our knowledge base, the competency to address dynamic situations reduces over time due to conflicting and irrelevant information.

For you to truly learn, you must first know how to unlearn. You must try your best to break out of the rigid chains of preconceived notions. You must first know the relevance and the need for any capabilities. Then, you need to do away with your old practices and old ways of working, which may not be applicable in the current context. You must try to retain only those that are relevant and useful in the recent scenario, and then, start learning and adopting new capabilities.

The 3R's of unlearning, namely REALIZE, REMOVE and RENEW, help in identifying your current capabilities and skills, eliminating unwanted ones, retaining useful ones and adding new capabilities. In this new way of learning, the learning, unlearning and relearning loop keeps repeating over and over, and the competency to address dynamic situations increases over time due to renewed and relevant information.

LEARNING AGILITY

Have you been in a situation where you felt that you could do something easily sometime back, but now you find it difficult or impossible to achieve? If you have been in such a situation, wouldn't you agree that these situations can make one feel ill and suffocated? Being trapped in such a situation, one would want to come out of it as soon as possible. But now, you may need more effort or resources to achieve the same feat that you could have easily achieved earlier.

Let us look at an example. As time passes by, you may find that the energy and tactics with which you have been managing and playing with kids earlier is completely lost now, and you are no longer able to manage a kid even for one hour. When this happens, remember one thing very clearly, this surely is not anything related to your age or the responsibilities that you carry. The main reason behind this is that as days pass by, you become unaware of the child's new needs and desires, and mistakenly, you use your old tactics of keeping the child engaged.

You may have heard the phrase "You have lost touch" being used very often. This just means that your notions have become outdated, and you are no longer familiar with the changes in your surroundings. Your speed of learning is much lower than the speed of changes that are happening around you. If you must remain relevant, then your speed of learning must be higher than the rate of changes. The learning curve must be above the change curve. But speed alone does not help. Speed with accuracy is essential for mastery. One must remember that with speed one is prone to making mistakes; thus, accuracy is a necessity to becoming a full-fledged master.

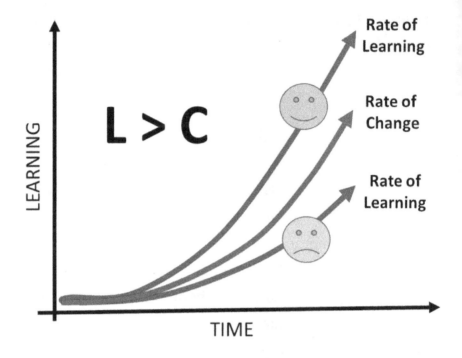

The ability of an individual to learn rapidly, respond and resolve an anticipated change by continuously reviewing and renewing their competency to perform is called **Learning Agility.**

LEARNING AGILITY = SPEED OF LEARNING × ACCURACY IN LEARNING

This can be applied at workplace while managing deliverables and teams as well as at home while managing household chores, relationships, health, self or anything else. Agility in learning the nuances of activities as well as understanding and applying that learning in the right manner is at the core of Personal Mastery.

5A's OF LEARNING CYCLE

The 5A's of learning cycle, namely AWARE, ACCEPT, ANALYZE, ALTER and APPLY, help to build and develop learning agility or learn the art of learning with increased speed and effectiveness.

1. AWARE — Reflect on current experience to establish a need to relearn to achieve performance.

2. ACCEPT — Acknowledge and identify the effort to learn and unlearn certain capabilities.

3. ANALYZE — Determine the strategies required to learn and unlearn the identified capabilities quickly.

4. ALTER — Develop empowering capabilities and dispose derailing capabilities.

5. APPLY — Deploy new capabilities to achieve expected performance.

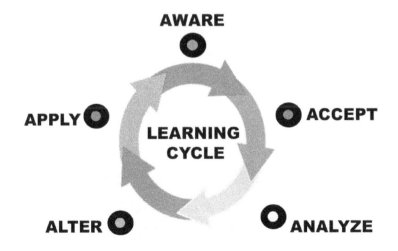

For one to move from good to great, it is necessary to be aware of the required changes and accept them. Unless this is done, it's not possible to master oneself. One must compete with multiple changes occurring every day to stay upgraded and ahead of the world. But mere acceptance and awareness will not help. It may be that you understand the changes that are needed and accept them, but it is possible that you don't know what to do and how to do it.

Similarly, just working on the changes due to external forces does not provide the desired results. It must be well understood, intrinsic and deep within. Individuals with high learning agility quickly adapt to changes and spend maximum effort (up to 80%) on ALTER and APPLY, whereas individuals with low learning agility consume enormous effort on ACCEPTANCE to change, spending very little effort on actual implementation. They spend only 40% on ALTER and APPLY. The rigidity in awareness and acceptance to change becomes a bottleneck, which needs to be removed to master or transform oneself.

Chapter 4

AAR for Continuous Learning

TRIPLE LOOP LEARNING

You might have experienced that sometimes things are so easy and uncomplicated that you feel like you are living a happy dream. You get all the desired results, and everything happens as you expected. But you may not experience the same desired results the next time, and the outcome may be different each time. You may now think that you were probably lucky the first time, and hence, you might not worry about finding what got you there.

At the same time, you might have also come across instances where every time the outcome is predictable and similar. Is it that you got lucky every time? Is it possible?

In the first case, you are unaware of how you achieved the desired outcome. Hence, the next time the outcome may be different. Whereas in the second case, you have reflected upon your actions, and you are completely aware of what drives the outcome; hence, you achieve the same or similar outcomes every time. Reflecting on all actions is the key. It is not only important to reflect on failure, but also equally or more important to reflect on your success. Ultimately, you must be aware of why you are successful or why you are not successful. This will help you in repeating and achieving the desired outcome time and again.

"Learning from experience, however, can be complicated. It can be much more difficult to learn from success than from failure. If we fail, we think carefully about the precise cause. Success can indiscriminately reinforce all our prior actions."

– N. R. Narayana Murthy

Let us do a small exercise.

Two teams — Team A and Team B — were identified and both were invited for a session. Team A attended the same session four times. Team B attended the session only once, but they participated in three rounds of brainstorming sessions. A week later, both the teams were tested on their learning. Team B scored 50% higher than Team A. Team B studied one-fourth as much as Team A yet learned far more than Team A. What did Team B do differently?

Each time they went in for a brainstorming session, they reflected on their understanding, made course corrections and became aware of their learnings. Whereas Team A learnt the same thing repeatedly without making any changes that were required.

We can apply the same concept in our daily actions and bring the awareness and reflections to our actions. In our everyday life, we come across various situations and actions, and for every action, there will be an associated outcome and reaction. This reveals our behavior in or response to any situation, and it happens in all instances. Here, you are unaware of the reasons behind your actions, and you may continue to behave the same way in such situations irrespective of whether it is right or not. This is single loop learning.

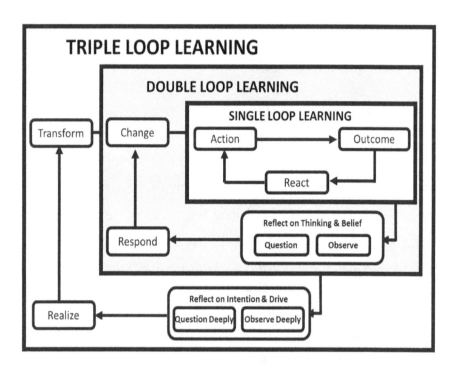

Now, if you start observing and questioning your actions, you will reflect on your behavior and the cause. Here, you are aware of the reasons behind your actions, and thereby you can choose to respond or not. You will have complete control on your actions, and therefore, your behavior can change simultaneously by reflecting on the actions. This is double loop learning.

While reflection on your actions certainly help you change, this will still not guarantee you the desired results every time. There is something deeper than just your actions and behavior, which are your intention and drive. Start questioning your drive and intentions and observing them deeply. This process will enable you to not only respond, but also realize and eventually transform. Transformation will bring in permanent change in you. This is Triple Loop Learning. This is the ultimate realization and deep learning when the truth of life starts unveiling its secrets in front of you. Personal discovery is all about discovering your drive and desire through triple loop learning.

"The importance of repetition until automaticity cannot be overstated. Repetition is the key to learning."

– John Wooden

Per the triple loop learning model, we must reflect repeatedly and not just once. The process of discovering the drive must repeat for every action every time. Once you begin repeating and reproducing consistently, it becomes a habit. Once it becomes a part of your daily life, you will no longer feel the process.

AFTER ACTION REVIEW (AAR)

In double and triple loop learning, we learnt the way of reflections and the need to repeat and reproduce consistently, until it becomes a habit. Habits are the only way by which a person can stick to certain rules. But these internal changes alone will not help. It is more important for the changes to be visible outside. Changes that are externally visible to the world are indicators of and testimonies to what you have learnt from your experiences.

Change happens due to three primary reasons:

- You have been HURT ENOUGH so now you want to move away from the misery and change for your good.

- You have been HAPPY ENOUGH so now you want to explore more and change so that your happiness is permanent.

- You have LEARNT ENOUGH from your experiences and as a result you have been able to reflect on your actions, realize the impact of your actions, and hence, you feel the need for change.

In the first two cases, you want to change as soon as possible, but you may not know how to change. Whereas in the third case, your experiences have enabled you to understand why and how you want to change. You will have a clear idea about why you crave for the transformation. This will be a continuous learning process, which can be accomplished via the **After Action Review (AAR)** process.

AAR is a structured process that gives you a guideline to achieve change smoothly. It is a continuous learning tool that involves reflecting on a particular action, learning from it and improving thereon. Whenever you come across an incident/situation, conduct AAR as soon as possible so that you can recollect and reflect on the various actions that were undertaken. If only you were involved, then conduct on self; if it is a team, then involve all the stakeholders.

Top five questions to be answered:

1. **What was supposed to happen or expected to happen?** What was the plan here and what were you expecting based on your execution plan?

2. **What happened in reality?** Was this in line with your expectations or better than what you expected or worse than what you expected?

3. **Why did 'what happened'/the unexpected happen?** Perform critical analysis here and start reflecting to understand and unearth the reasons for the unexpected outcome. It is quite possible that many a times this stops at the THINKING or BELIEF level. But you need to reflect deeper to analyze the INTENTIONS and DRIVE behind these actions.

4. **What is the learning from the outcome/result of this incident?** What are the learnings that you would like to take forward?

5. **What will you do now based on the learning?** Once you have this reflection, realization and learning on why 'what happened' happened, you will start thinking on how you can change to make the next incident better. What should you be doing more of to make things work? What you should be doing less of so that things don't fall apart? What you should start doing newly from now on? Finally, what you should stop doing from now on?

No matter what the process is, there is a need to record and measure everything. If you don't record, you won't have a proper benchmark to measure your progress, and you won't have any accountability to meet them. Most of the stringent goals of large corporates or the national goals are publicized, even if they are aspirational goals, as this drives commitment and motivation to meet them, and thus, it makes you responsible for meeting the targets. Record your AAR and the changes you want to make and share the findings with others.

This process provides you with the ability to transform for the better. Next time when you say or believe you have changed, then immediately answer these four questions:

i) What are you indulging more into? ii) What are you doing less of? iii) What new good things have you started doing? iv) What old incorrect/inefficient things have you stopped doing completely? If you do not have proper answers to these questions, then you have failed to implement the change.

"A real decision is measured by the fact that you have taken a new action. If there is no action, you haven't truly decided."

– Tony Robbins

AFTER ACTION REVIEW (AAR)

INCIDENT	1. WHAT WAS SUPPOSED TO HAPPEN?
2. WHAT ACTUALLY HAPPENED?	3. WHY "WHAT HAPPENED" HAPPEN?

4. WHAT CAN YOU LEARN FRON THIS OUTCOME / RESULT ?

5. BASED ON THE "LEARNINGS" WHAT SHOULD YOU ....

DO MORE OF....	DO LESS OF....
START DOING....	STOP DOING....

Summary

AAR helps you examine and enhance **personal capabilities** and implement them in your day-to-day activities and life. The more time and energy you put into the right kind of practice, the longer you stay in the deep learning zone and the more transformed individual you become.

Chapter 5

3S's for Individual Performance

*"Working hard for something we don't care about
is called stress; working hard for something we love
is called as passion."*

– Simon Sinek

When we look around us, we can find several examples of successful individuals such as Bill Gates, Steve Jobs, The Beatles, Sachin Tendulkar, and many more. Here is how successful people are described typically: they worked really hard, they just got lucky, they were born talented, they are gifted, they have high ambition, they have better IQ and so on. We think so because we only see the result: Olympic gold medalist, world champion, successful businessman, etc.

What we fail to recognize and notice is their years of commitment, their willingness and desire to achieve, their continuous learning journey, their daily discipline and their consistent practice with a purpose that helped them achieve individual excellence.

No one becomes successful overnight. No one gets successful with just one song. No one gets successful with just one century in a cricket match. For example, all of us know that Bill Gates is one of the richest men in the world, but what we don't know is how he got there. At the age of 13 years, he put in 1,500 hours and seven months of coding and learning on a machine. For the next seven years, he did not take a single day off and worked 12 hours a day, for all 365 days. Only then did he become successful.

So, what makes an individual so successful? We have learnt in previous chapters how learning and building relationships drive performance and results. But by applying these principles and tools, would we see consistent results across all individuals? Can we declare without any doubt that by adopting these ways any individual can achieve excellence and be successful?

We see several universities and corporations across the world that use strong objective criteria for onboarding individuals onto their institutions or enterprises. Then, they put them through streamlined, repeatable and reproducible processes that align with the six sigma standards. As all of them are given the best training available, they are naturally expected to work efficiently. Now, when these individuals are put on a job/assignment, do they all perform the same way? If this situation is ever achieved, it would be an ideal state. But we all know it's not true, and there are always few people who perform better than others, given that all other factors are almost the same.

Let us take an example that every one of you can easily relate to. You must have observed that the food prepared by a cook and the food prepared by your mother have a huge difference in taste even though both are equally competent and follow almost the same steps.

What drives this differentiation in the above two cases? It is the WILL that drives this differentiation. For any individual to achieve extraordinary performance, they should have both the right will and the right skills. The desired results are not produced by only one of these two essential qualities. Individuals fail if they have only skill or only will. Your mother has both the skills and the will to prepare food, whereas your cook has only the skills and would do it as a service or as an obligation for the money paid. Similarly, the high performing talent in the organization possess the skill, techniques and the unwavering passion that differentiates them from other talents who may have similar skills but less passion and will. When skill and will are combined for the right purpose, then the individual becomes extremely powerful.

Let us look at another example, this time from martial arts. Whenever I watch martial arts, I see exceptional and consistent performances. The warriors are extraordinary. All of them have a strict regimen, and as a result, they acquire unwavering determination. But how do they do it?

When I researched a little more, I discovered that a warrior must possess three key ingredients: first, the SPIRIT, which means the desire or will to do something; second, the STYLE, which is the skill, process and steps; third, the SWORD, which is the tool for fighting. The sword is given only after the warrior masters the style (skill). A true warrior always seeks the right sprit, the right style, and the right sword — in that precise order.

If they just have the right spirit (will) but not right style (skill/process/steps) and sword (tool), then they get killed. If they have the right sword but not the right spirit or style, they still get killed. Either way, a martial arts student must never deviate from the strict decorum set for them. During learning, they emphasize and enable students to first have the right sprit, followed by the right style and, finally, the right sword. Similarly, for an individual to achieve excellence, it is important to have the right will (spirit), the right skill (style), and the right tool (sword). These are the basic ingredients of any individual learning and performance.

Spirit can be the individual's belief, drive, mindset, willingness to perform the job and other similar qualities.

Style is the various skills required for the job, including individuals' learnings, experiences, various methodologies and processes, guidelines, do's and don'ts, etc.

3S

Model of Individual Excellence

Spirit

**Individual
Excellence**

Sword   Style

Sword is the resources required to do the job efficiently and effectively, including tools, aids, measurement index, and feedback and control mechanisms to review the performance.

Summary

An individual will perform to their maximum potential if they possess the right sprit, style and sword. When all three are perfectly balanced, only then they will be able to achieve Individual Excellence.

Chapter 6

2R's for Sustainable Performance

"We can improve our relationships with others by leaps and bounds if we become encouragers instead of critics."

– Joyce Meyer

We often hear that successful people can achieve balance in all aspects of life — both professional and personal. We wonder if this is all about being planned, prioritizing tasks and managing time and energy. Or is there something more?

Humans are social beings, and good relationships with family, relatives, friends and the society are essential aspects of a fulfilling life. Our mantra is that balancing the 2R's of PERFORMANCE — Relationships driving Results — is the key to extraordinary and sustainable performance.

This principle applies to both personal and professional lives. At the workplace, there are multiple stakeholders — clients, manager, subordinates, peers, colleagues in support functions, etc. YOU are at the center of all of them. Maintaining harmony in all these relationships is essential for extraordinary performance.

If you want to be an extraordinary person, you need to first realize that you cannot do everything on your own. You need to actively connect with people and seek the right support from the right stakeholders at the right times. For this to work harmoniously, building intimate relationships is essential. Intimate relationships go beyond knowing a person. The foundation is built by mutual respect, acceptance, appreciation and trust. Only when these are firmly established, we can harness each other's support and transform into extraordinary performers. When you focus on building these strong bonds with the people you work with, you not only contribute to your own growth but also to the growth of everyone in your circle.

Now, how do we achieve and maintain these intimate relationships at the workplace where we don't necessarily have personal connections to begin with? To do this, we present to you the five spirits of relationship building.

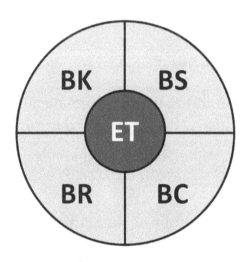

ET — Earn the Trust of your people through your actions, not words. Earning trust is at the core of any relationship. This is gained from your actions of sincerity, care, respect and knowledge.

BK — Be Knowledgeable about your people's backgrounds, likes, dislikes, strengths, weaknesses, aspirations, etc.

BS — Be Sincere with your people about your intentions and interests.

BC — Be Caring about your people's welfare and future before your own.

BR – Be Respectful of your people's positions, beliefs and values always.

If you want to understand where you stand with respect to your current relationships, ask yourself and answer the following two questions:

How well do you **KNOW THEM?** Cordially or intimately.

How much do you **CARE FOR THEM?** Superficially or deeply.

Family relationships are usually intimate and deep. You can elevate workplace relationships to the intimate and deep level by taking simple steps. For example, a team member falls sick:

Surface-level interaction — Asking them if they are fine.

Deep-level interaction — Ensuring they get checked up, proactively asking them what help and support you can provide and following up with actions.

All you need to do is put in a little extra effort and treat them like family. That's the real difference. When your team member sees that you sincerely care about their well-being, they will appreciate your efforts and trust you a little more for it. The relationship will develop positively.

Let us delve deeper into this process of transforming relationships from 'surface–cordial' to 'deep–intimate' type of relationship. The technique we have developed for this purpose is the FIVE STEP RELATIONSHIP STAIRCASE. It is important that you understand the process and apply all these steps in your actions. This method will help you measure and build sustainable and intimate relationships.

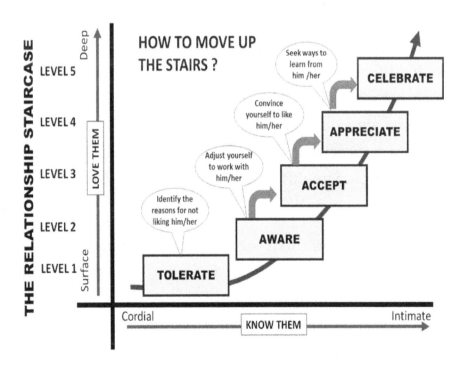

In any relationship, it is imperative to understand that the individuals are unique and different from each other. The objective is to preserve the uniqueness and build the relationship without harming the individuality. It is a fact that we all have differences and relationships need to be built despite these differences.

Level 1 — TOLERATE

At the first level, you TOLERATE the difference. When any two individuals come together, gaps in understanding occur not because of what is common, but because of what is different. We never fight over common things; we always fight over different things.

So, at level one, you identify the differences, the reasons behind them and tolerate them. Many times, we don't even know why we don't like another person. Therefore, you must remain calm and think clearly how you can get rid of the negativity arising due to differences. The objective here is not to eliminate differences, but to identify and tolerate them.

Example: You don't like the way your peer presents their points during a review. You feel that they boast about themselves and believe they are always right. You do not express your criticism in public, instead you tolerate and listen attentively and make notes on your feedback (likes and dislikes). Then you can speak to them privately and express your feedback points in a calm and composed manner. This will open an opportunity to know them better.

Level 2 — AWARE

The second level is being AWARE of the differences. There will always be differences between individuals, you understand them and gain awareness of the reasons behind these differences. Then you start adjusting to work with them accordingly, without expecting them to adjust with you.

Example (continued): You know what you do not like about your peer's presentation. You have discussed your feedback and will not be affected by their way of presenting in future reviews.

Level 3 — ACCEPT

At the third level, you ACCEPT the differences. Now that you know the reasons for the differences, you will respect and accept the differences and convince yourself to like them. This is something that you must program within yourself, not others. You must be the one to initiate the boost in the relationship.

Example (continued): You will work with your peer closely to understand their points of view and keep this conversation going.

Level 4 — APPRECIATE

At the fourth level, you APPRECIATE the differences. You will start finding out why you are not able to do what others are doing. Now, you can not only tolerate and accept, but you also know why you are doing something, and why others are different. As a result, you start appreciating and learning from them. You must always remember that every individual has the right to have a separate set of characteristics and beliefs just like yourself. So, respecting each other's choices holds priority.

Example (continued): You will start exploring with your peer the style of their presentation and find things to learn from them.

Level 5 — CELEBRATE

Finally, you CELEBRATE the differences. This can be done in two ways. Either you also adapt to their way of thinking, or you are completely convinced about your stand to remain different and justify others' differences. Celebration is always done together. So, when you are at the level of celebration, your relation is intimate and deep.

Example (continued): You will appreciate their strengths and request them to share their best practices and start implementing them, or you choose not to pick up any of their methods but sincerely appreciate their style of presentation.

The following planner will help you identify the current relationship level and chart out a path to move up the ladder. Once you identify the current level, put down the actions needed to move to the next level and the expected outcome for each level. Always try to progress forward and avoid being stagnant. As soon as you start respecting everyone's choices, you will be able to successfully climb up the relationship ladder.

"DEVELOPING & ENHANCING RELATIONSHIP" PLAN

PERSON	REASON

LEVEL	MY RELATIONSHIP IMPROVEMENT ACTIONS	EXPECTED OUTCOME
5		
4		
3		
2		
1		

Summary

Extraordinary performers operate in a state where Results are driven by **relationships**. Building relationship is all about how fast you can move up the ladder from tolerate to celebrate. You may sometimes fall to a lower level, but you need to quickly understand, get up and continue to move up. Best relationships always operate at the celebrate level.

Chapter 7

6:3:1 for 'Blame' to 'Ownership'

In our lives, we come across several people who are equally talented, in the fields of acting, music or sports, for instance. All of them start off extremely well, but not many reach the pinnacle despite having equal opportunities, mentorship, logistics and support. When we observe carefully, we notice that the reasons that elevated someone to the top are primarily their discipline and taking complete charge of their own actions. So, what is the motivation behind taking complete charge?

Over the years, we have engaged with various organizations. We have often heard leaders citing their team, their organization's processes and policies, their peers, their clients and many others as reasons for their failure. And these organizations invest heavily on defining organization structure with well-defined roles and responsibilities to bring more clarity to activities and ownership.

However, we have not seen significant success from these alone, as everything cannot be documented and defined. There will be some areas with clear ownership, some with shared ownership and some areas with no ownership. This is exactly the time when the BLAME game starts. This is where an individual does not own their actions and conveniently pushes back on any assigned activity citing numerous constraints, or the individual starts delegating every activity to others to solve the problem, or they start taking responsibility for everything and set themselves up for failure. None of these approaches help. Neither is everything our direct responsibility, nor is it prudent to assign everything to others.

So, how do you build a more scientific culture, where individuals, teams and leaders start taking more ownership automatically without blaming others?

Before we get into the scientific model, let us conduct a small exercise. Read the paragraph below in 15 seconds and identify the number of times the letter 'f' has been repeated.

Franco is a farmer from France. Over the last few months, four of his staff have forced him to lose one of his firm beliefs that fat people are very lazy. Of the four staff Freddy was the fattest weighing four hundred and fifty-four pounds. While many of the workers were frightened by Freddy's feverish eating habits, few dared to approach him and correct it. One of the reasons is they fear for their own safety.

There are 33 f's in this paragraph. Did you get your answer right? Now, read it again in 15 seconds.

__F__ranco is a __F__armer __F__rom __F__rance. Over the last __F__ew months, __F__our o__F__ his sta__FF__ have __F__orced him to lose one o__F__ his __F__irm belie__F__s that __F__at people are very lazy. O__F__ the __F__our sta__FF__ __F__reddy was the __F__attest weighing __F__our hundred and __F__i__F__ty-__F__our pounds. While many o__F__ the workers were __F__rightened by __F__reddy's __F__everish eating habits, __F__ew dared to approach him and correct it. One o__F__ the reasons is they __F__ear __F__or their own sa__F__ety.

Why did you not get it right the first time? Often the reasons cited will be:

- The time duration given was very short.

- The font was not very clear.

- If the f's were highlighted and underlined earlier, it would have been easier to identify.

- I could have asked my friend to read half the paragraph and read the other half myself to complete in 15 seconds.

- I did not pay attention, but I will pay complete attention next time to get it right in the stipulated 15 seconds.

#1. The first three reasons are your **actions of concern** (COMPLAIN) — You tend to find reasons and give excuses why you could not do what you were told to do. The focus shifts away from the problem to 'why I cannot do', and you start complaining citing numerous constraints and meaninglessly focus on how other factors should be addressed to solve it.

#2. The fourth reason is your **action of influence** (PARTICIPATE) — You still want to do it, but you believe that you alone cannot do it in 15 seconds and need others to be involved in the problem solving for better results.

#3. The last one is your **action of control** (FIX IT) — You understand where you went wrong, you know that you are the owner, and you fix the problem yourself.

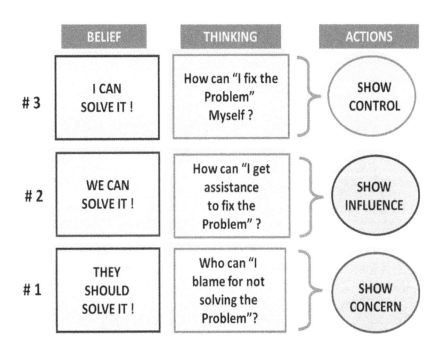

This can be well represented by the three spheres of action, namely CONCERN, INFLUENCE and CONTROL.

- CONTROL — Something you are worried about but can handle it all by yourself.

- INFLUENCE — Something you are worried about, and you need to work together with others to handle it.

- CONCERN — Something you are worried about, but you believe you can do nothing about it.

Individuals who fall in the #1 category are the BLAMERS, poor learning individuals who spend time and effort in finding faults and feel powerless most of the time. They believe 60% of the actions are to be owned by others, 30% of the actions can be performed jointly with some assistance, and they own only 10% of actions.

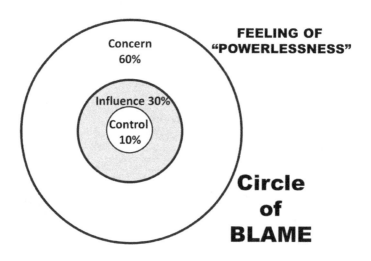

If we have 90% of our actions depending completely or partially on others, then we have NO CONTROL ON OUR LIFE. Is this how we want our precious life to be dealt with? Being completely controlled by others? Surely, none of us want it this way. To take charge of our situations and life, we must expand the sphere of control and become EMPOWERED individuals by focusing on 'What I can do' and not 'What others must do.'

An **EXCELLENT** performer can achieve the best possible performance **BECAUSE OF** various favorable reasons, whereas an **EXTRAORDINARY** performer can achieve the best possible performance **IN SPITE OF** numerous constraints.

Individuals falling in the #3 category are EMPOWERED individuals who believe 60% of the actions are to be owned and fixed by themselves, 30% of the actions can be done jointly in participative mode with some assistance and only 10% of actions are controlled by others where suggestions can be provided.

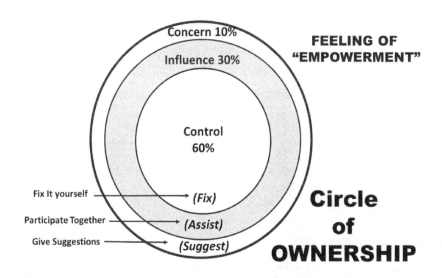

Let us now examine how to take charge of situations in every activity and become an extraordinary individual. The 6:3:1 rule helps individuals and teams to move from BLAME to OWNERSHIP. Prepare a chart of action items and categorize them under **concern, influence** and **control**. Not more than 10% of actions should be under **concern** and not more than 30% under **influence**. Maximize the actions under **control**, with a minimum of 60% of actions in this category. This will **empower** you to take complete charge of your life and situations and become **extraordinary**.

#	Actions to be taken	Expected Outcome	Due Date	Responsibility	Status / Corrective Actions
CONTROL	60%				
INFLUENCE	30%				
CONCERN	10%				

Summary

EXTRAORDINARY performance can be achieved only when one takes charge of situations and takes complete ownership of actions, irrespective of the constraints. The 6:3:1 ownership model is very helpful in managing personal challenges and changes. The 6:3:1 rule of ownership when implemented in every situation will clear ambiguity and latency and create long-lasting, impactful performances.

6:3:1 ACTION PLANNER

SITUATION

6

3

1

FIX THESE MYSELF

WORK WITH OTHERS TO FIX

SUGGESTIONS FOR

Chapter 8

PBS for Life's Four Demands

"We can change our lives. We can do, have,
and be exactly what we wish."

– Tony Robbins

Now that you have learnt how to master your life and control your actions to be directed according to your inner desire or drive, it's time to start implementing this in every aspect of your life.

As an individual, the priority for you is to be **happy** and **healthy**. These are the basic necessities that let an individual enjoy the positivity of life. Only when you are happy you are motivated to do anything beyond. A person who is not happy within cannot keep others happy. Being happy from within will help one to radiate positive vibes all around. At the same time, you must remember that you cannot be happy just by thinking about yourself all the time. There is something beyond self.

A person can never survive alone in the huge wide world. There is a society where you live in. You are a part of it, and you will definitely not be happy if you are not a good citizen of the society and contributing your bit. Then you have your family — father, mother, spouse, children, friends, etc. When you see your family and loved ones suffering, you cannot be happy. You always wish to be a good father, mother, son, daughter, husband or wife, and will remain unhappy if you are unable to perform any of these roles properly.

Similarly, you have a job and company with which you are associated with. It can be an NGO, self-owned business, social service, an employee in a company or anything. Your work environment needs to be conducive to hone your skills and must be reliable for you to grow.

These four aspects — SELF, FAMILY, SOCIETY and COMPANY — become life's four important demands. But how do you decide which is more important and what needs focus at any point of time? Will you be happy just by focusing on one of these at any point of time? Can you ignore the rest and deprioritize? NO! Not at all! You cannot remain happy just by focusing on any one of these. Very soon the next demand will become a critical one to address. You need to balance all the four demands of life equally and devote attention. But is balancing all four possible? Does it sound theoretical to you? Let us help you with a tool that provides a mechanism to understand, follow and succeed in balancing life's four demands.

PERSONAL BALANCE SCORECARD (PBS)

The first step towards this is to understand and gather the needs and expectations from **self, family, society** and **company**. These needs and expectations will be your KPIs (key performance indicators) based on which you will work on your performance plan. You can either talk to others to gather these or you can write them down yourself.

- **SWOT analysis** — Now that you have your expectations clear, conduct a personal SWOT analysis. Identify your strengths, weaknesses, opportunities and threats. Start reflecting on your thoughts — what makes you happy about yourself and what makes you unhappy about yourself. This will give you an insight into your current reality.

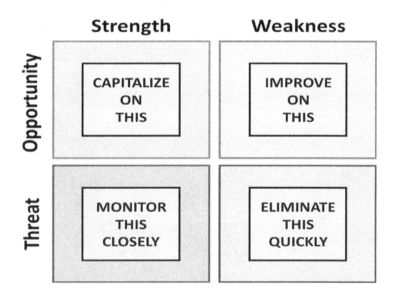

- **SMART goals** — Before you start penning down the various goals, priorities and plans, you will need to understand how to define them. Apply SMART principles for every goal/activity that you define.

  - **S**pecific — Clear goals with well-defined actions

  - **M**easurable — Quantifiable and able to be monitored

  - **A**chievable — Realistic

  - **R**ewarding — Encouraging with each milestone achieved

  - **T**ime bound — Dated

Now you can start drafting your scorecard. The PBS has two important components, DIRECTION and ACTIONS. Direction constitutes your **drive, intent (purpose), goals/ vision, belief, thinking,** etc. and **actions** constitute the key actions that you will undertake to meet these while balancing the four demands of your life. Write down your answers to the following questions in each category.

DIRECTION

1. **Purpose** — This will be the core intent, drive that answers questions such as 'Why are you in existence? What can make you remembered for long? What will give you a noble purpose, meaning and passion in your life?

A sample answer: To improve the quality of lives of people living in my village.

2. **Vision** — Where do you see yourself in 10 years from now? How should society view you with respect to your contributions? How should your family see you in terms of your relationship with them? How should your company view your performance and capabilities?

   A sample answer: To be a successful entrepreneur providing employment opportunities to at least 40,000 people.

3. **Three years' mission** — What do you want to achieve in the next three to four years that will bring you closer to your vision?

   o **External** — This is what you achieve that can be seen from the outside (what would be visible to others): material achievements, physical achievements, financial achievements and career achievements.

      A sample answer: To be recognized as Best Manager by my organization.

   o **Internal** — This is what you achieve on the inside, and only you can feel this: inner peace and joy, sense of harmony with the world, sense of accomplishment and sense of worth.

A sample answer: At workplace, to improve my **relationship** ladder quotient from **'tolerate'** to **'celebrate'** status in next 12 months with all my subordinates.

4. **Value proposition** — What kind of **'character'** person you want to be so that you can add value to your company, team, family and society?

"The true test of a man's character is what he does when no one is watching."

– John Wooden

5. **Beliefs** — What should your **"intentions and drives"** be so that you can build your **character** and **values**? INTENTION can be to serve the nation, to have fun in life, to do a quality job, to make every customer happy. DRIVE can be joy, love, revenge, power, anger, grief, etc.

6. **Key programs** — List down the **make-or-break** programs that you must do, such as all urgent and important things. And make sure to identify those. Break away from not urgent and unimportant things.

7. **Key performance areas** — Identify the performance index parameters on key areas such as friends, emotional state (good, bad, poor), health, competencies and financial status.

Now that you have set the **direction** and understand WHAT you want to achieve, WHY you want to achieve, for WHOM you want to do it and WHERE you want to be in a specific period, it's time to get determined and start thinking on HOW you want to achieve all these.

Identify all projects/actions that you will be undertaking over next 12 months to achieve the performance areas set in your DIRECTION. Be cognizant of the basic ground rules and tools such as 6:3:1 Ownership model, triple loop learning and AAR principles. For every action, do not forget to define the target completion date, ways to monitor the progress and ways to measure the outcome. List down all the contributors who will be part of this plan.

ACTIONS

8. **Social** — Include five things that brings pride and five things that cause shame to society, how do you pay back to society, and so on. For example: Number of rules/laws violated, number of voluntary service actions performed.

9. **Family** — Include things that you will give back to family, areas of responsibilities, etc. Days of family celebrations per month, number of appreciation letters/gifts for family members, hours of family conversation per week, number of good friends, etc.

10. **Career** — Consider areas like alignment of self to organization goals, capability development etc., number of competency gaps addressed, number of innovations suggested/accepted, number of customer appreciations, number of hours spent on team engagement, number of performance feedback sessions held, number of work projects completed, etc.

11. **Wellness** — Goals on your health, wealth and stress levels such as hours of exercise per week, total savings per month, amount of investment, number of days spent on your hobbies, etc.

12. **Learning** — "Training is what others can give you, Learning is what you can give yourself." So, focus on self-learning areas such as number of books read on any topics of your choice, number of articles submitted, number of areas you applied your learnings this week and number of people you coached/mentored.

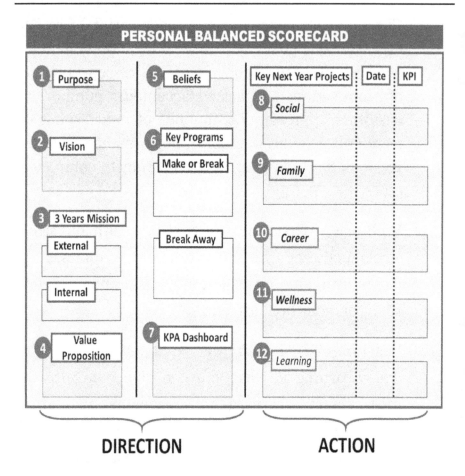

As soon as you finish chalking out a proper plan, get ready to make it public with people you love, value or respect — your spouse, mentor, parents, true friend, supervisor (for career-related actions) and so on. This will make you more accountable for the actions you have listed, help monitor your progress regularly and provide you an opportunity to seek help when needed.

Once you have publicized the plan, there is no going back. The main difference between successful people and others is their NEVER GIVE UP attitude, even when it's boring, painful and time consuming. Remember the following to make it an executable and successful plan.

1. There is no middle path to any of these actions, and there is no 'trying'. It must be DO or DO NOT.

2. Break the actions into multiple sub-actions so that you see progress in several small milestones.

3. Speed is of the essence. Fix target dates and always meet them no matter what.

4. Have belief in self and make steady progress.

5. 'Doing is learning and learning is doing.' Learn all through your life, enjoy the journey of experiential learning, reflect on your actions and implement innovative ideas on these.

6. Finally, celebrate every milestone. You deserve it!

Summary

All the knowledge you have gained is worthless if you do not apply it. It's time to transform yourself by taking actions from your learnings. PBS is the most important conceptual tool, which serves you as a lifelong learning log. It captures all your thoughts and is extremely efficient when used regularly.

Part 3

Extending Personal Transformation Principles to Team and Organizational Performance

Chapter 9

Performance Formula for Organizations

"The future of performance management in organizations is going to be more and more about the performance of the network of people you are working with as opposed to the performance of you as an individual."

– Alex Shootman

Through the preceding chapters, we have covered the concepts of deep learning and how they influence our actions and performance. Now that we have mastered the self, it is time put these learnings into practice. We are always part of some group — family, friends, team, organization — and our actions and performance will have profound impact on these groups.

"A nation prospers when its people prosper." Similarly, an organization performs only when its people perform. People are assets for any organization. People determine the customer experience, people build solutions, people enhance work culture, people drive innovation and people inspire other people. Every individual has a role to play in an organization — an entry-level executive, a line manager, an executive leader, CEO and so on. Every performance is a cog in the wheel; every performance is like a brick in the grand set up of an organization.

*"An organization's ability to learn, and translate that
learning into action rapidly, is the ultimate
competitive advantage."*

– Jack Welch

Organization is a group of individuals collectively working towards one larger objective. A **learning organization** is a group of people working together in such a way that they're continually enhancing their capabilities both individually and collectively to create performances consistent with their deepest aspirations. Imagine a team of dedicated, loyal employees, who are all focused on their own personal transformation and learning. What would such a team ultimately deliver?

Team performance

*"Organizations learn only through individuals who learn.
Individual learning does not guarantee organizational
learning. But without it no organizational learning occurs."*

– Peter Senge

Learning is not about one person. Everyone in a team or in an organization must learn. If one learns fast and many others learn slowly, the net effect is that the whole organization learns slowly. For example, say an employee can render a given scope of work within 10 minutes. Another employee can do it within 20 minutes. A third employee takes

30 minutes to deliver the same. Collectively, when this organization (of three) works together, the speed of the team (the performance factor) is reduced to the speed of the mediocre or that of the slowest. The rate of organizational performance can only be enhanced when everyone learns and performs at the same rate.

Learning should not happen for the sake of learning. Learning must happen for the sake of performance. Learning should not be regarded as part of our daily chores and nice to have; instead, it must be internalized as the fundamental instrument for survival; it is a MUST-DO matter. As CEOs and CIOs, it is critical that learning is duly equated with detailed ROIs. It is also necessary to evaluate how much they spend (on learning) and how much they gain.

Learning must start from the self. At this stage, it is all about passion. It is about the passion to excel in whatever an individual chooses to do or is assigned to do. From this dimension of individual learning, the learning process must grow into the scale of a team (more than one member). Learning, then, needs to transcend beyond a single team. It should pervade across many teams without boundaries. Teams must be aware and accept the changes that happen around them.

How teams respond to these changes is what constitutes real learning. Teams must actively seek for answers within and across teams to survive changes and their implications. With the lessons and answers sought, teams must be nimble enough to alter and act accordingly. Teams must be continually orientated to increase capabilities and capacities. Teams should transform themselves into LEARNING TEAMS, and no matter how successful they are or appear to be based on immediate achievements, they MUST NOT stop learning.

A team's performance can be mapped based on a maturity matrix combining five components with two criteria each. The five components and their corresponding criteria of extraordinary teams are as follows:

1. GOALS — which are **shared** and **progressive**

2. LEADERS — who are **inspiring** and **system thinkers**

3. FOLLOWERS — who are **committed** and **innovative**

4. PROCESSES — which are **mutually agreed** and **improvement orientated**

5. CULTURE — based on **performance** and **continuous learning**

"Great things in business are never done by one person; they're done by a team of people."

– Steve Jobs

Organizational performance

When we extend the science of individual performance to learning teams and further to organizations, it is a healthy combination of the right resources (Re), the right processes (Pr), and the right people (Pe). People's mindsets and attitudes are becoming the cornerstone of organizational performance, and there is a strong need to innovate and continually change and enhance their skills to bring about outstanding performance, especially with the Gen-Y workforce.

It was annual performance evaluation period in my organization and everyone was busy in charting down their accomplishments for the year. During this period, I had my management guru visit my organization for audit and assessment. As part of the assessment, he joined me for one of my team members' performance feedback evaluation. During the discussion, I demonstrated a lot of management leadership principles, such as **authority**, **assertiveness** and **quantitative** performance evaluation, and gave my subordinate a strong message for his inability to meet the goals and suggested improvement areas to meet them. I was hoping to receive appreciation from my guru for implementing the management principles; instead, I was taken aback with the question asking for the reason for my unruly and aggressive behavior with my subordinate. I tried justifying with explanation on top-down goals and the mandate we have at all levels to meet, which otherwise would impact the organization scorecard, etc., but he stopped me there and further probed me on the real **intention** behind this behavior. By this time, I had become aware of the answer — it was an act of revenge for the pain and agony that I went through during my performance evaluation by my managers, where I was bashed for my team's poor performance.

He then told me something that is beyond management definitions and principles:

"True leadership is about showing love, giving hope and having faith and not about hate, fear and revenge."

Bottom-line–driven performance competencies (tools, processes, systems) are no longer enough on their own to ensure high and sustainable organizational performance. To achieve sustainable performance, you need a leader who steers the direction of the team towards the organizational goals through project and team goals. The leader works against the constraints and achieves outcomes with the spirit of IN-SPITE-OF. They perform AAR, document and extract new (emerging) knowledge matters and share them with their teams and across other teams. Leaders (Ld) have an exponential impact on organizational performance. Following this logic, we have derived a formula for organizational performance as follows:

$$(Re + Pr + Pe)^{Ld} = \text{Organizational Performance}$$

PERFORMANCE FORMULA

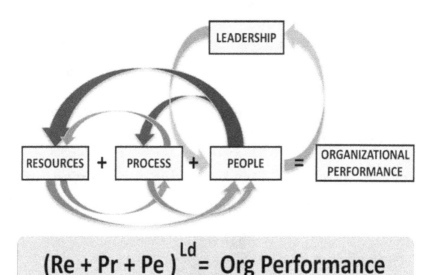

$$(Re + Pr + Pe)^{Ld} = \text{Org Performance}$$

However, the challenge for leaders is to manage resources, processes and people in a way that brings about lasting growth. But people are the most complex and the hardest to manage. How powerfully and effectively the general inspires and trains his army to use weapons, resources and strategies directly affects the outcome of the battle. Leaders need to rise and ensure they influence the culture and values of their people as well.

If any one of these parameters goes beyond the control of a leader, the desired performance may not materialize. It is meaningless if an organization has the most expensive resources and sophisticated processes but have people who have reached stagnation in their learning. Good people must be hired and developed through the right capacity and capability-building facilitations. Good people with the right attitude of performance must be also equally rewarded. People need strategic recognitions and inducements to continue performing without lapses. People cannot or should not be managed. People can only be inspired. Leaders who have mastered self will drive **team** and **organizational** transformation and performance to greater heights.

"Coming together is a beginning. Keeping together is progress. Working together is success."

– Henry Ford

9 798886 415759